# Pebble® Plus

## ZOO ANIMAL MYSTERIES

# A Masked Mob Mystery

by Martha E. H. Rustad

**Consulting Editor:** Gail Saunders-Smith, PhD

**Consultant:** Jackie Gai, DVM
Zoo and Exotic Animal Consultant

CAPSTONE PRESS
a capstone imprint

Pebble Plus is published by Capstone Press,
151 Good Counsel Drive, P.O. Box 669, Mankato, Minnesota 56002.
www.capstonepub.com

032010
005740CGF10

Books published by Capstone Press are manufactured with paper
containing at least 10 percent post-consumer waste.

*Library of Congress Cataloging-in-Publication Data*
Rustad, Martha E. H. (Martha Elizabeth Hillman), 1975–
    A masked mob mystery : a zoo animal mystery / by Martha E.H. Rustad.
        p. cm.—(Pebble plus. Zoo animal mysteries)
    Includes bibliographical references and index.
    Summary: "Simple text and full-color photographs present a mystery zoo animal, one feature at a time, until its
identity is revealed"—Provided by publisher.
    ISBN 978-1-4296-4497-6 (library binding)
    1. Meerkat—Juvenile literature.  I. Title. II. Series.

QL737.C235S85 2011
599.74'2—dc22                                                2010001349

**Editorial Credits**
Jenny Marks, editor; Heidi Thompson, designer; Svetlana Zhurkin, media researcher; Eric Manske,
        production specialist

**Photo Credits**
iStockphoto/Brandon Laufenberg, cover; Douwlina Boshoff, 7; Rainer Schmittchen, 18–19
Peter Arnold/Martin Harvey, 8–9
San-Maré Pretorius, 12–13
Shutterstock/Dmitry Pichugin, 4–5; EcoPrint, 21; Jacek Jasinski, 11; John Arnold, 14–15; Mark Beckwith, 17

# Note to Parents and Teachers

The Zoo Animal Mystery set supports national science standards related to life science. This
book describes and illustrates meerkats. The images support early readers in understanding
the text. The repetition of words and phrases helps early readers learn new words. This book
also introduces early readers to subject-specific vocabulary words, which are defined in the
Glossary section. Early readers may need assistance to read some words and to use the Table of
Contents, Glossary, Read More, Internet Sites, and Index sections of the book.

# Table of Contents

This book is about a mystery zoo animal. That animal is me! If I give you clues, can you guess what I am?

Here's your first hint: In the wild, you'll find me in the hot Kalahari Desert of Africa.

Where I Live

North America

Europe

Asia

Africa

South America

Australia

Antarctica

5

# Dirty Digging

To keep cool, I live underground.

I dig tunnels as deep

as 7 feet (2.1 meters).

The deeper I dig,

the cooler my home will be.

To dig my tunnels,

I use my long front claws.

They scratch through

the hard desert ground.

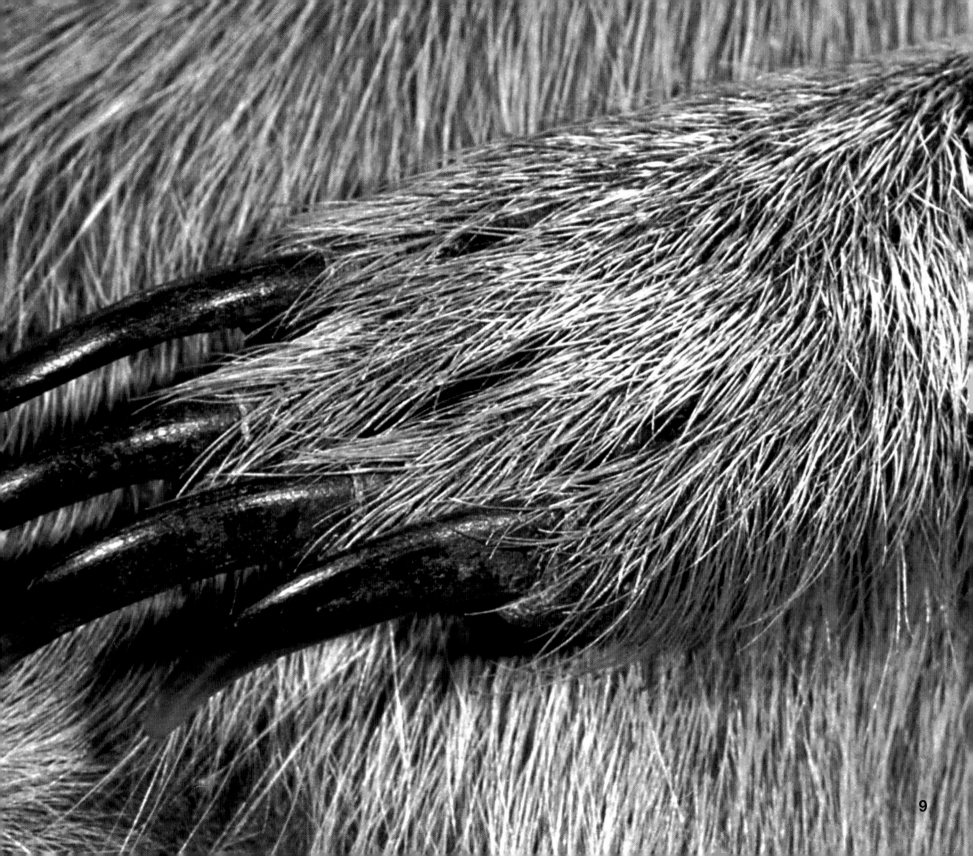

9

# My Life and Kids

My family of eight lives
together in our burrow.
We snuggle together
in a big furry pile.

Once or twice each year,

my mate and I

have a litter of pups.

Our pups' eyes stay shut

for about 10 days.

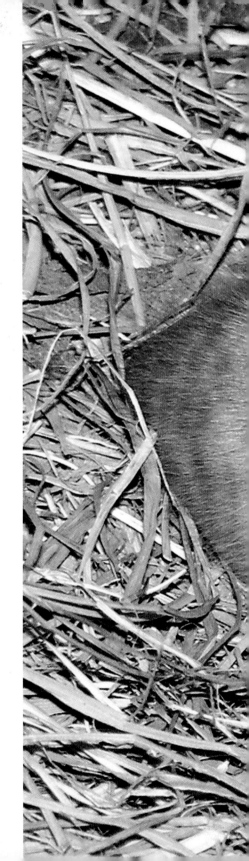

My family takes turns
watching for predators.
We stand up straight and
balance with our long tails.
If we see trouble, we bark!

## Sight and Smell

When it's time to eat,

I sniff and dig deep.

My good sense of smell

helps me find prey.

I eat insects and scorpions.

Dark rings around my eyes
block the bright desert sunlight.
I can close my ears tight
to keep out the sand.

Have you guessed what I am?

# Mystery Solved!

I'm a meerkat!

This zoo mystery is solved.

# Glossary

**burrow**—a hole or tunnel in the ground made by an animal

**insect**—a small animal with a hard outer shell, six legs, three body sections, and two antennas

**litter**—a group of animals born at the same time to the same mother

**mate**—the male or female partner of a pair of animals

**predator**—an animal that hunts other animals for food

**prey**—an animal hunted by another animal for food

**pup**—a young meerkat

# Read More

**Rake, Jody Sullivan.** *Meerkats.* African Animals. Mankato, Minn.: Capstone Press, 2008.

**Storad, Conrad J.** *Meerkats.* Early Bird Nature Books. Minneapolis: Lerner, 2007.

**Walden, Katherine.** *Meerkats.* Safari Animals. New York: PowerKids Press, 2009.

# Internet Sites

FactHound offers a safe, fun way to find Internet sites related to this book. All of the sites on FactHound have been researched by our staff.

Here's all you do:

Visit *www.facthound.com*

Type in this code: 9781429644976

# Index

Word Count: 205
Grade: 1
Early-Intervention Level: 16